#AuntAlma:

Raisin' a Little ~~Hell~~ Heaven on Earth

ADRIENNE ROSS
Illustrated by John Morgan

Copyright © 2016 Adrienne Ross

All rights reserved.

No part of this publication may be reproduced, stored in a retrieval system, or transmitted in any form or by any means, electronic, mechanical, photocopying, recording, or otherwise, without the prior written permission of the author.

Published by:
ARC Publishing
P.O. Box 173
Jackson, MO 63755

ISBN-13: 978-0692707630

ISBN-10: 0692707638

For **Alma Ross**,
whose humor has enriched my life,
and whose faith in God and in me have helped mold me into the person I have become.
I wrote them down, but your words, wit, and wisdom authored this book.

ACKNOWLEDGMENTS

I could not have completed this project without the support of people who believed #AuntAlma was worth it.

First, I thank my Savior, Jesus Christ, who both birthed and fueled every passion and gift I possess. I am nothing without Him.

I thank my family for being the constant in my life. Your love is unconditional, and contrary to the adage, I know I *can* always come home again. We do not see each other all the time, and we have our share of battles when we do, but we're family, and when push comes to shove, we've got each other covered. Thank you for loving me.

Thank you, Facebook family. It started with you. Your love for my aunt inspired me. You're the ones who encouraged me to share her stories. You're the ones who laughed with the words she spoke. You're the ones who said, "Write a book." You're the ones who made her heart soar when I finally told her there were people out there who had never met her, but loved her nonetheless. Every person who offered a Facebook "share," "like," and laugh, thank you. Every person who ordered a T-shirt, a mug, or a pen with #AuntAlma's image, thank you. Those who recorded video messages to her or took selfies with merchandise you purchased, thank you. Everyone who embraced my aunt as your own, thank you. I could not have done this without you.

Kristi King, my lil sis, thank you for being my sounding board through every aspect of every #AuntAlma project. I counted on your keen eye for details, your feedback when I was clueless, and your unending patience with my ranting about it all. You designed and mailed out merchandise, which paved the way for where things are today. Your handprint is on all of everything that is #AuntAlma. You always believe the best in me and for me, and you're always cheering me on. Thank you!

Elysia King, my first illustrator, you're amazing. The image you created was the image people first associated with #AuntAlma. They fell in love with that sassy woman you drew, knowing you had captured her spirit. Thank you for bringing her to life.

John Morgan, you're the man! Your incredible artistic talent took #AuntAlma to the next level. Thank you for being my illustrator. You took #AuntAlma from one image to many, as you infused her quotes with her attitude. You were flexible, hard-working, and invested in this project. I appreciate you and what we created together.

Martha Cano, without a doubt, you were #AuntAlma's biggest supporter. You purchased every design, which helped me believe the project was worthwhile. You're the best. Thank you!

Even if I did not mention your name, please know that every person who has been a part of this process—with hands on or just with kind words—is special to me and an integral part of this book. May God reward and bless you. I thank you so very much.

INTRODUCTION

Alma Louise Ross was born in Timmonsville, South Carolina, in 1937. Her birth certificate says she was born on July 7, but she says it was July 2, and that's when we've always celebrated it. Well, that day and July 4—because the 4th of July is just a good excuse to celebrate anything: you've already got the hotdogs, hamburgers, and sausages. Might as well add a cake and sing "Happy Birthday." Auntie says there's a good reason her birth certificate says the 7th: "Down South, when people said second, they thought you said seven, so they wrote seven." Well, okay.

Aunt Alma is one of two of my dad's sisters. Growing up, my sister, Marion, and I loved spending time with Auntie, as we still call her. She was our favorite aunt—the funny one, the one who brought the goodies, the one who would let us stay up late and wouldn't make us wake up early. You know, the cool aunt. Later, when my brother, Andrew, was born, she was his Auntie, too.

Her sister, my aunt Mary, was the stern one. Okay, I'm being gentle; she was the mean one. But that's because she always had to take care of everyone—practically raising my dad and Aunt Alma. She brought responsibility and stability to the table. Aunt Alma brought candy and cupcakes. So any chance we got to hang with Auntie was a little Heaven on Earth.

In this book, readers will hear, in her own words, her take on the world—and trust me, she's got something to say about everything—and she doesn't mind saying it. Some of it is such common sense wisdom, you have to go, "Well, yeah!" Some of it just leaves you scratching your head, and you can't help but say, "Huh?!" Much of her wisdom is laced with references to God and the Bible, and a good measure of the hell—uh, Heaven—she raises occurs under the steeple of her church, where she's attended for more than 50 years. Yep, even the church isn't safe from her wit and wisdom. I imagine there are times the members wish they were. As my aunt sees it, however, she's not raisin' hell, nor would she ever—because, as she has told us, "Ain't nobody in Heaven raisin' hell."

And she fully intends to get into Heaven.

So how exactly did this #AuntAlma movement start? It really was quite effortless. During our conversations, she is sure to say something funny or absurd or just classic—whether the "Well, yeah" variety or the "Huh?!" sort. I started sharing some of these on Facebook. People found her funny, yet wise. Some said she reminded them of an aunt of their own or a grandmother. Others were just downright tickled. They latched onto her and adopted her as their own. Requests for T-shirts and mugs came. Can you imagine? I met this demand by hiring someone, and then someone else, to design them, and people actually bought them. It really was as simple as that.

I never told her of her Facebook fame until some time later, but the demand for her grew: "Give us more #AuntAlma." People were hungry for her sarcasm, her sass, her simple wisdom—all wrapped up in her unique brand of humor.

Now, we all have #AuntAlma at our fingertips in this collection of some of her quotations interspersed with real-life stories about everyone's favorite aunt.

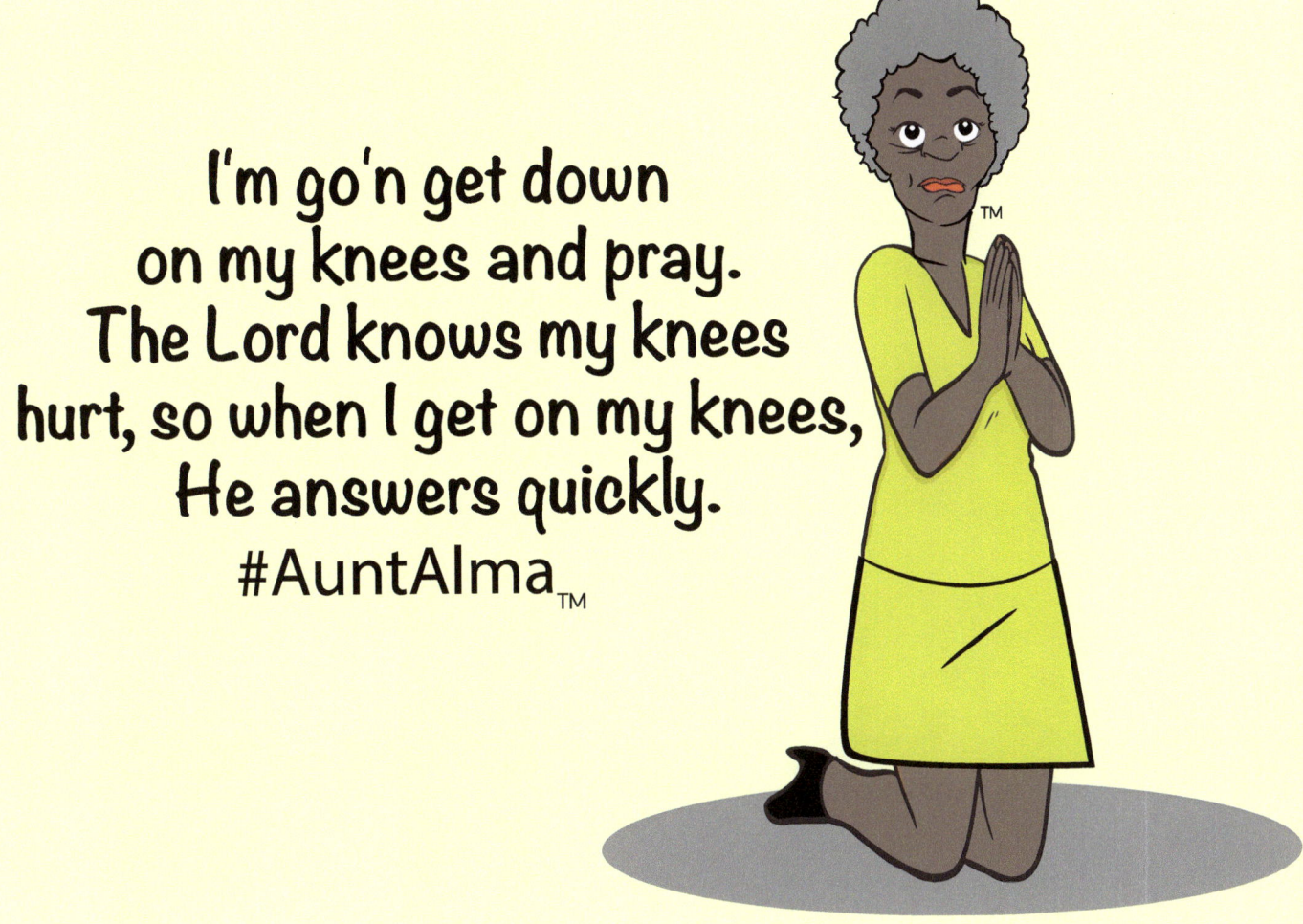

She's my friend, but she can't be trusted. She'll steal your drawers off you if you don't pull 'em tight! #AuntAlma

Aunt Alma often shares the story of how her big sister, my aunt Mary, would say to her, "Alma, you're scared of *everything*!" As these pages reveal, Aunt Alma is a woman of faith in God and a faithful member of her church. But that does not mean she's not willing to take some matters into her own hands, whether that means going to the doctor several times a week—just in case—or avoiding an airplane flight because she's not sure what God's will is and doesn't know if she'll arrive safely from Point A to Point B.

She'll tell you, however—and I know it's true—that if she absolutely has to get on that plane, she'll get on. If I need her, for example, she'll be there. So she may be "scared of everything," and she may not "know what God's will is," but when it comes to the people she loves, she'll take her chances, pray for the best, tell the pilot to "step on it!" and talk to anyone on the way who will listen.

You'll hear more about aging, sickness, funerals, and doctor's appointments in a five-minute conversation with Aunt Alma than one should in a lifetime. I've talked to friends with aging relatives, and I've learned that this is not at all uncommon. I guess when people you've known for years are passing away, and you're battling your own aches and pains, you start to think a little more about eternity than you used to.

The thing about my aunt, though, is her preoccupation with physical frailty and the afterlife are often so funny, you can't help but laugh, especially when she makes plans to live until she's at least 150 years old while simultaneously declaring she's not afraid to die since others have done it successfully!

I ain't afraid to die. Everybody else do it; I can do it, too!
#AuntAlma™

I don't wanna see none of y'all once you die. Don't come see me, and don't send nobody else to see me, either!
#AuntAlma

Folks talkin' 'bout when they get to Heaven, they go'n look for loved ones who died already. I'm only looking for one person when I get to Heaven--and His name is Jesus! I ain't looking for nobody else. And don't expect me to come back and visit y'all. I ain't coming back to see nobody. #AuntAlma™

My arms are getting flabby. I could get rid of it, but I can't go to the gym no twice a day; I'm tired. So I'll have to be a little flabby, and cover it up, and go on 'bout my bi'ness.
#AuntAlma

I was thinkin' 'bout living till I am 950-years-old like Noah in the Bible, but at this point, I'd better just take 150 and shut up!
#AuntAlma™

Aunt Alma is a fixture in her church. She's been there for a lifetime, and she hardly ever misses a service. Judging from stories she tells me, I'm sure there are times when folks at church wish she went on vacation—for their sake, not hers! They count on her for many things, so they probably don't want her to go away too long, but a short break would be welcomed, I bet.

Since she's convinced she ain't raisin' no hell, I don't want to disrupt her delusion with truth, so I go along with it. The truth is she's a trip! From Bible studies to meetings, from revivals to church dinners, she's got her hand—and mouth—in everything. Sometimes, she manages to keep her mouth shut, but with eyes rolled, hands on hips, and leg stuck out, she can still tell it like she sees it without uttering a word. Most of the time, she's got plenty to say, though, so her mouth is always at the ready.

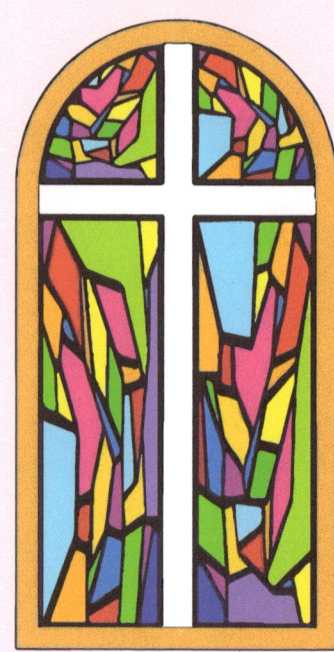

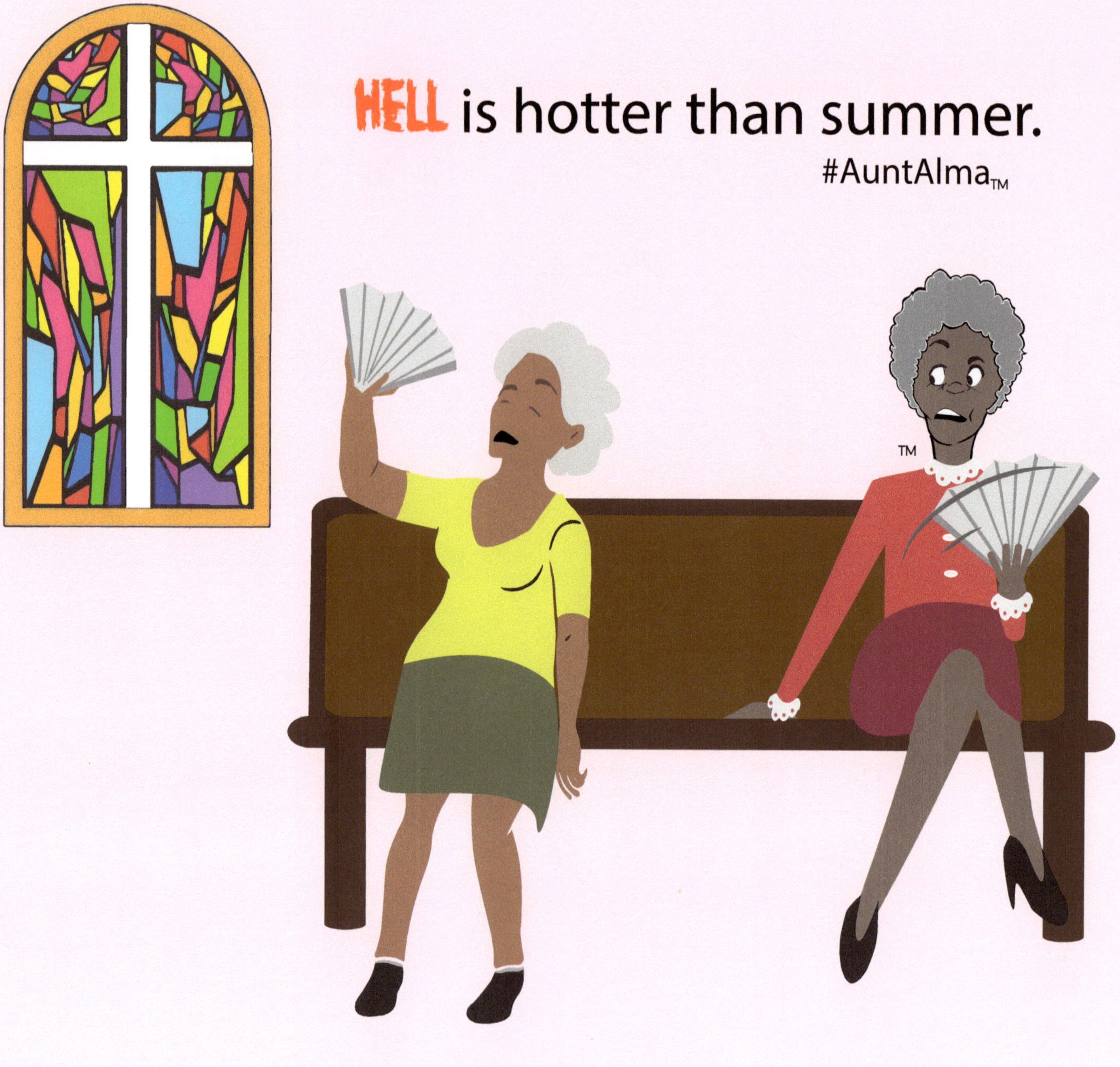
HELL is hotter than summer.
#AuntAlma TM
TM

She wanna pretend the Spirit gets on her every Sunday--making her jump and shout on me! I told her if she stomps on my foot one mo' time, I'm go'n knock her out. Funny how since then, she shouts all 'round me, but ain't touched me one time.
#AuntAlma™

Just because you're getting old doesn't mean you can't look good. My aunt is not one to dress up just to hang around the house, but when it's time for church or some other event beyond piddling around at home or running errands, oh, you best believe she'll be looking good. Her friends say, "You don't have to worry about Alma; she'll be dressed right." And that's the truth. She'll be late getting there, and she'll have to stop to pick up some pantyhose on the way, but when it's all said and done, she'll be looking good.

That's a redeeming quality for someone whose daily activities slightly resemble a *Carol Burnett Show* episode. Growing up, it was common to hear, first thing in the morning, awaking me out of sleep, "Adren," which, for some strange reason, is how she pronounces my name. "Adren, you know what I'm looking for?"

Arghh!!! I would think. *Here we go again!*

"Adren! You know what I'm looking for?" she'd repeat. I'd reach for the pillow to put over my head or the blanket to scoot down deep underneath. But neither was enough, as she would ask another question to answer the previous question I had not answered: "Where's my other shoe?"

Unable to escape, I would crawl out of bed and search the possible places she could have left her shoe. Once I found it, the next thing I'd hear might be, "Adren, you seen my pocketbook?"

Ughh! The search was on for her pocketbook.

"I hope I didn't leave it in the car," she'd say.

Just wait. Here it comes—in five, four, three, two, one: "You seen my car keys?"

I'm not lying. I'm not even exaggerating. "Alma Ross, played by Carol Burnett" could easily be in the credits of her life—or even "Carol Burnett, played by Alma Ross." But nobody was playing anybody; this was real—and it was daily.

Not much has changed all these years later. I'm an adult now, but when I visit her, I'm still called upon to search for shoes, purses, and keys. We can just add a cell phone to the list—something we didn't have to concern ourselves with all those years ago.

Who would think that someone that scattered could step out and look so good on so many occasions, but she did—and she does. Now, if she's going to the post office or the grocery store, she's got a flimsy hat thrown on her head, jeans that are much too big, and sneakers my sister gave her when she no longer wanted them. Come Sunday, however, it's a different kind of hat—one befitting Sunday School teacher/church choir president/Missionary Alma Ross. Well-ironed skirts and dry-cleaned dresses. High-heel shoes and high-class steppin'. On Sunday, she's struttin', but because she's getting on in age, she's had to alter her strut. After all, she says, "When you get old, you gotta walk a certain way so you don't fall down."

When you get old, you gotta walk a certain way so you don't fall down. You gotta throw your head back and up in the air, point your toes out, stick your behind out, and go on 'bout your bi'ness.
#AuntAlma

She died at 90, and they're saying she lived a long life. People in the Bible lived 900 years, so I'm trying to make it to at least 150. #AuntAlma™

It's a good day! Ain't nothing gone wrong yet, and I ain't expecting it to!
#AuntAlma

The Spirit didn't knock me down. That man knocked me down!
#AuntAlma™

Aunt Alma was never an animal lover, until she found herself with animals—two dogs that belonged to her sister. When Aunt Mary got sick and Aunt Alma pretty much moved in to help my uncle take care of her, she also took care of the dogs, the mom-and-daughter combo of Shirley and Tiny, respectively. She bought special food for them and cooked it. Yes, I said she bought food that she had to cook! She treated them better than most humans get treated. Still does. She even talks to them like they're human. The fact that they have special needs only makes her even more protective. These dogs are allergic to everything. They can't eat this. They can't eat that. They must have special food and snacks, which, come to think of it, is just like her, with the special diet she requires because of what she calls "my sugar." In case you don't know, "sugar" is diabetes.

Both Aunt Mary and Uncle Cleveland eventually passed away, and Shirley and Tiny went home to Aunt Alma's house and continued their diva status. We should all be so fortunate as to have the kind of care these two get. And they absolutely love her. They stay under her, will hardly let anyone near her, and pace the floor or stare out the window when she leaves, awaiting her return.

No wonder her friends say those dogs have the best gig going, one they wouldn't mind having—even if they have to die to get it.

My friends say
when they die, they wanna come
back as one of my dogs!
#AuntAlma™

That DEVIL is trying to get me--trying to make me get confused, and go to sleep, and not get my Sunday School lesson I gotta teach. He ain't go'n get me tonight!
#AuntAlma

Some people have a gift for working with young people, and some have a gift for working with elderly people. Rarely do we encounter those who do both with equal ease. Aunt Alma does. In her church, she teaches Sunday School to teenagers and is also a missionary who spends a lot of time with the elderly and sick. As my brother says, "Auntie is either in the graveyard or the hospital."

She believes in helping those who don't have family—baking a sweet potato pie to bring to someone on Thanksgiving and visiting sick folks to pray for them; that's Missionary Ross for you, as they call her at church.

She invests quality time in the young'uns, too, trying to deposit some godly wisdom and life lessons into them. Sometimes, it seems daunting, as it's no small task in this social media age to capture young people's attention, much less their hearts. But she does, sharing one nugget after another. They love her, which fuels the fire in her belly to help them however she can. The combination of a sharp tongue and a sweet spirit keeps them appreciating Aunt Alma. She's a bit of a pushover, I think, but she insists there's a limit: "Once you tear yo' tail with me, I'm done," I've often heard her say. "Tear yo' tail" translates to act a fool, do her dirty, blow it big time. I've never seen her reach her limit, though many surely should have passed that limit by now. She runs her mouth and talks tough, but she always comes through. Oh, don't get me wrong: if you "tear yo' tail," she'll talk bad about you—but she'll also be there for you.

Every time I tell you I might get married one day, you say, "Well, good for you, but Jesus is MY lover." Don't be sayin' that too loud. They go'n get the wrong idea and lock you up.
AuntAlma™

As common as losing items is for Aunt Alma, even more common is a broken-down car. Something is always wrong with her car. So even in her 70s, she'll walk to church, take a bus to the store, or stay home—anything but buy a new car or take her car to a mechanic who will fix it right and send her on her way quickly. Instead, she either leaves it parked on the street in front of the house or takes it to her mechanic friend, who doesn't work on cars as often as he used to and will get to it when he gets a chance. All too often, she goes out to start the car and "it won't crank," as she says, or it does crank but breaks down somewhere.

I visited her for Thanksgiving in 2014, and she drove it to her early-morning church service. Andrew, my brother, told her to take his car instead because he had no intention of going to get her if her car broke down. But, no! His car is too fancy for her, and she can't figure it out, so she insisted on driving her own car. Sure enough, the phone rang a couple hours later, and she needed Andrew to come jumpstart her car. He complained, but he went.

Instead of coming home after he got her car going, she went on some other Thanksgiving morning errand. Andrew returned home. The phone rang after a while, and Andrew announced he was not going to get her. With some insistence on my part, he relented and went to get her, complaining. I certainly couldn't blame him; his car was sitting in the yard and he had offered it, but she refused. Now, she was calling upon him to run all over creation to "crank" her car.

This happens repeatedly. That crazy car! I visited her for Thanksgiving in 2015 also, and her car was acting just as crazy as the year before; I took her to her friend's shop to pick it up after it was repaired. The only problem was it *wasn't* repaired, so before I left New York, she was back to leaving it parked on the street.

Just get a new car, Auntie.

And a new cell phone.

It was hard enough, I suppose, for her to get a cell phone at all, so I shouldn't push it, but when your phone innards are showing, it's time. She progressed to getting a phone that's intact, but she's not yet ready for one that is modern because…well, *she's* not modern. She still can't quite figure out how to check her voicemail or turn the volume down while she's at church or even remember where she put it most of the time.

Once, she allowed a cell phone sales representative to sell her a touch screen. When she told me, I was scared for her! I knew it would not end well. I knew it would not even begin well. Long story short, after a painful trial period, the sales rep took back the phone she bought during that delusional moment and managed to get her out of there with an older woman's dream—an old-fashioned flip phone without the bells and whistles.

Aunt Alma is ever the optimist, so she talks big about one day getting a modern phone, a tablet, and a computer so she can "fax." Do I think it'll ever happen? Well, since what she calls fax is actually email, I'm not so confident. I often consider buying her a tablet or laptop, but I always decide against it because I know if I do, it'll sit there unused, just like the NutriBullet blender I got her for Christmas. She wanted it to make smoothies (and to puree salmon!), but she did nothing with it. Instead, she waited for me to come visit, almost a year later, from

19 hours away so I could "put it together" for her. Putting it together amounted to screwing on the blender cup.

No, Auntie is not the most modern woman, but maybe that's what makes her special. She stays grounded in who she is and from where she came. It may drive the rest of us crazy, but somehow, she manages to survive—making us laugh a whole lot on the journey.

I need a new cellular phone. The guts are falling outta this one, so I tied my stockings 'round it.
#Aunt Alma

Sure, God will forgive us and let us go to Heaven, but we may catch hell on the way there!
#AuntAlma

ABOUT THE AUTHOR

Adrienne Ross is an editor, writer, public speaker, online radio show host, and former teacher and coach. She spent her entire career in education teaching English Language Arts in Hudson, New York, a career that spanned more than 17 years. She began a new chapter in her life in October 2013, moving on from teaching and relocating to Missouri.

She is the owner of Adrienne Ross Communications and has been a speaker and panelist at churches, youth events, school assemblies, and political functions, and has written for politicians, public figures, newspapers, and websites.

Through life's challenges, Adrienne has learned the power of perseverance through faith and hope. As a Christian, she believes God has given everyone a unique calling, and she encourages people to pursue their purpose.

If you or your group is interested in purchasing this book in bulk or scheduling Adrienne Ross to speak at your event or conference, please contact her at **adriennerosscom@gmail.com**.

Visit Adrienne Ross's website at **http://www.adriennerosscom.com/**.

ARC Publishing
P.O. Box 173
Jackson, MO 63755

www.ingramcontent.com/pod-product-compliance
Lightning Source LLC
Chambersburg PA
CBHW061357090426
42743CB00002B/49